W9-ARL-172

THE FACTS ON ROCK MUSIC

John Ankerberg & John Weldon

HARVEST HOUSE PUBLISHERS
Eugene, Oregon 97402

Other books by John Ankerberg and John Weldon

The Facts on Astrology
The Facts on Creation vs. Evolution
The Facts on the Faith Movement
The Facts on False Teaching in the Church
The Facts on Hinduism
The Facts on Holistic Health and the New Medicine
The Facts on Islam
The Facts on the Jehovah's Witnesses
The Facts on Jesus the Messiah
The Facts on Life After Death
The Facts on the Masonic Lodge
The Facts on the Mind Sciences
The Facts on the Mormon Church
The Facts on the New Age Movement
The Facts on the Occult
The Facts on Roman Catholicism
The Facts on Sex Education
The Facts on Spirit Guides
The Facts on UFOs and Other Supernatural Phenomena

This booklet is a revision of the authors'
Rock Music's Powerful Messages (Part 1)
© Ankerberg Theological Research Institute, 1991.

THE FACTS ON ROCK MUSIC

Copyright © 1992 by The Ankerberg Theological
  Research Institute
Published by Harvest House Publishers
Eugene, Oregon 97402

ISBN 0-89081-974-2

CONTENTS

– 1 –

How Powerful Is Rock Music?

For changing people's manners and altering their customs, there is nothing better than music.

Shu Ching, Sixth Century, B.C.

Rock isn't what it used to be; it has changed. Writing in *U.S. News and World Report*, David Gergen comments, "The difference between music of yesteryear and that of today is the leap one makes from swimsuits in *Sports Illustrated* to the centerfolds of *Hustler*."[1] Joseph Stuessy of the University of Texas, one of the first professors to teach a course on rock music, has said, "There is a new element in this music which was not a part of Chuck Barry, Buddy Holly, or John, Paul, George, and Ringo. That element seems to be a meanness of spirit."[2]

Rock today is a worldwide force with hundreds of millions of fans. For many, it is their personal religion. The earlier endorsement of drugs, sex, and rebellion remain, but new themes have been added such as violence, nihilism, escapism, and the occult, making rock more controversial.

Many people don't know how to think about the conflicting viewpoints that surround rock music today. Some say, "It's dangerous." Others disagree. Still others say, "It's just a passing fad," or "Scientific studies have never proven it harmful," or "After all, kids never listen to the lyrics anyway, so how can they influence them?"

How does one sort out these issues? We hope this introduction to rock music, in conjunction with our video material,[3] will be useful in helping you do this.*

History's Verdict on the Power of Music

To begin with, few who have studied music will deny that it has power to influence and dramatically affect our lives.

---

* This booklet can stand alone or be used with our TV series, "Rock Music's Powerful Messages," which provides supplemental documentation and discussion. See note 3 for ordering information.

It is perhaps the most effective mood-setter there is. In his book *On Heroes, Hero-Worship and the Heroic in History*, Thomas Carlyle mused, "Who is there that, in logical words, can express the effect music has on us? It is a kind of inarticulate, unfathomable speech, which leads us to the edge of the Infinite, and lets us for moments gaze into that!"[4] Anatole France once commented that "songs have overthrown kings and empires."[5] And in his *Darwin, Marx, Wagner*, Columbia University historian Jacques Barzun, author of *Pleasures of Music* (1951), refers to "the power of music to embody with precision certain parts of the human experience which no other art can express."[6]

In *The Merchant of Venice*, Shakespeare argued, "The man that hath no music in himself, nor is not moved with concord of sweet sounds, is fit for treasons, stratagems, and spoils; the motions of his spirit are dull as night, and his affections dark as Erebus. Let no such man be trusted."[7]

The great German reformer, Martin Luther stated, "I have no pleasure in any man who despises music. It is no invention of ours; it is the gift of God. I place it next to theology."[8]

Even the skeptical philosopher Nietzsche commented in his *Twilight of the Idols*, "Without music, life would be an error."[9]

The great and famous down through history have all agreed music does have power and that power can be used for either good or evil. This is why Dr. Howard Hansen, former director of the Eastman School of Music, commented in the *American Journal of Psychiatry*, volume 99, p. 317, "Music is a curiously subtle art with innumerable varying emotional connotations. It is made up of many ingredients, and according to the proportions of these components, it can be soothing or invigorating, ennobling, or vulgarizing, philosophical or orgiastic. It has powers for evil as well as for good."

Today's rock musicians testify they, too, are aware of the power of their medium. For example, Frank Zappa in a *Life* magazine article has said, "The ways in which sound affects the human organism are myriad and subtle.... *The loud sounds* and bright lights of today *are tremendous indoctrination tools*."[10]

Mickey Hart, drummer for the Grateful Dead, states, "*Sound is an incredible force* that can transmit feelings through the physical extension of sound waves and their fractions in length and amplitude."[11]

Slash, the lead guitarist for Guns n' Roses declares, "I mean, this is serious. It's [my music] affecting the lives of people you don't even know, which is definitely a scary thing, *to have that much power*" (emphasis added in all quotations).[12]

Hal Ziegler, one of the first big promoters of rock entertainment during the 50's comments, "I realized that this music got through to the youngsters because the big beat matched the great rhythms of the human body. I knew it and I knew there was nothing that anyone could do to knock that out of them. I further knew that they would carry this with them the rest of their lives."[13]

Knowing they have this power rock musicians unhesitatingly beam their concerts worldwide in behalf of various causes such as world hunger, farm assistance, AIDS, etc., because they are confident they will be able to influence people's behavior.

Further demonstrations of the power of rock music are the two largest media events in history. The largest media event ever was the United Nation's worldwide broadcasting of John Lennon's record, "Imagine," in honor of the anniversary of his death. The second largest event was rock's "Live Aid" concert for the starving people in Ethiopia. Notice that both of these media events featured rock music.

Also, everyone knows that large corporations pay millions of dollars for 30-second television ads which specifically utilize music. They believe these ads will affect and motivate our behavior and persuade us to buy their products. For example, Ray Charles sings about Pepsi, "You've got the right one, Baby." Or Delta Airline's melodious jingle, "We love to fly and it shows." Toyota implants in our minds the lyrics, "Oh, I love what you do for me—Toyota!"

Of course, advertisers do more than play jingles; they combine their music with great visual pictures. Rock music does the same. Catchy beats and powerful, entertaining imagery can't help but convey messages more effectively. But this brings up another controversy.

The U.S. government has passed laws banning visual pictures of child pornography. Why? Because the government believes sexually explicit pictures have a profound effect on human minds and behavior. If they are correct, then what about the visual pictures seen by millions at rock concerts and on music television? Are these pictures of human sexuality, although less blatant, without effect?

The power of music is real. And those in media know that what people see and hear does affect them.*

---

* Examine the videos that accompany this booklet. Do you think the visual and auditory messages displayed in these rock scenes have no power to influence people? (Cf. e.g., MTV's "10th Anniversary Special" aired on ABC, Nov. 27, 1991.)

Controversy over music is nothing new. Some 2500 years before Christ, the Egyptians had written their observations on papyri concerning the effects of music on mind, body, and emotions. Around 1000 B.C. the dramatic effects of King David's music on King Saul were noted in 1 Samuel 16. In the sixth century B.C. Pythagoras stated that music was a precise science able to exercise great influence upon the emotions and senses. Plato (427–347 B.C.) once demanded the censorship of certain kinds of music because he feared "citizens would be corrupted by weak and voluptuous errors and led to indulge in immoralizing emotions." In *The Republic* 424c he stated, "The introduction of a new kind of music must be shunned as imperiling the whole State; since styles of music are never disturbed without affecting the most important political institutions." In his *History of Music* Emil Neuman wrote, "He [Plato] insisted it was the paramount duty of the Legislature to suppress all music of an effeminate and lascivious character, and to encourage only that which was pure and dignified...."[14]

The noted philosopher Aristotle (384-322 B.C.) wrote the following concerning music in his *Politics*: "Emotions of any kind are produced by melody and rhythm" and "music has the power to form character," its arrangement being so important that "the various modes may be distinguished by their effects on character...one, for example, working the direction of melancholy, another of effeminacy; one encouraging abandonment, another self-control, another enthusiasm, and so on...."[15]

St. Clement of Alexandria (A.D. 150–220) emphasized, "It must be banned, this artificial music which injures souls and draws them into various states of feelings, sniveling, impure, and sensual, even a bacchic frenzy and madness."[16]

St. John Chrysostom (A.D. 347–407) argued, "It must be submitted to severe control and everything must be banished which recalls the cult of pagan gods...."[17] A.D. Amicus, M.S. Bothius (sixth century A.D.) observed in *De Institutione Musica*, "Music is a part of us and it either ennobles or degrades our behavior."[18] A.W. Tozer observed, "If you love and listen to the wrong kinds of music, your inner life will wither and die."[19]

Though controversy surrounding music is nothing new, what is required is sensible thinking on the subject. People in general, Christians included, should be expected to separate the wheat from the chaff in the areas of music just as in the areas of modern cinema, art, and literature (see Chapter 9). These, too, offer a mixture of good and evil and each individual must determine where to draw the line. For the

Christian, that line must be drawn on the basis of sound biblical principles.

The Effects of Rock Music

The effects of rock music on teens and preteens can no longer be ignored. Psychologists tell us that during the teenage years the adolescent value system is being molded and fixed, perhaps for all time. So it's important to ask what messages are being conveyed to teenagers who frequently listen to rock music four to six hours each day.[20] How will these messages influence and shape them?

Psychologists who research the effects of music have expressed concern: e.g., leading psychological researcher John Kappas' studies indicate that people "are truly susceptible to conscious messages on a record and that excitation and melancholy can be created by [musical/sensory] overload.... 'Any time you overload the mind, the person becomes very suggestible. They will take in anything that you suggest at that time because they have no defenses against it. People can walk out of concerts in a hypersuggestible state.... Music has a tendency to defuse thinking and create moods. And in turn, the messages seep in.'"[21]

The potential effects of certain forms of rock music are so serious that over a dozen states have now introduced legislation requiring rating or labeling of offensive music albums and videotapes.[22] According to *Time* (May 7, 1990) lawmakers in 19 states have considered proposing warning labels. Further, the National Parent Teacher's Association, the American Academy of Pediatrics, and the U.S. Surgeon General "have voiced concern over the negative influence this type of music has on children and adolescents."[23] Legislation submitted to the House of Representatives provides good examples of what people are concerned about:

First, "The media of music, lyrics and visual images, separately and especially in combination, have had a profound influence on society and its individual members for both good and ill from the beginning of recorded history."

Second, "Certain music and music videos promote negative thought and behavior by suggesting, advocating or encouraging violence, vandalism, rape, murder, drug abuse, suicide, human sacrifice, degradation of women, children and human life, bestiality, sadism, masochism and other perversions."

Third, "Such indecent and negative material too often targets youth in the impressionable teen and even pre-teen years."

And fourth, "Such material is almost universally available to anyone regardless of age with sufficient money...."[24]

Today, even the medical community is concerned about the negative effects of rock music on our youth. A study in the prestigious *Journal of the American Medical Association* (September 22, 1989), "Adolescents and Their Music: Insights into the Health of Adolescents," concluded:

During adolescence, teenagers are expected to develop standards of behavior and reconcile them with their perceptions of adult standards. In this context, music, a powerful medium in the lives of adolescents, offers conflicting values. The explicit sexual and violent lyrics of some forms of music often clash with the themes of abstinence and rational behavior promoted by adult society.... Physicians should be aware of the role of music in the lives of adolescents and use music preferences as clues to the emotional and mental health of adolescents.[25]

In *The Closing of the American Mind*, noted sociologist Allan Bloom also expressed concern over the influence of rock music on preteens, teenagers, and even college students.

Bloom argues that young teenagers who have emerging concepts of sexuality are not allowed to develop normally. Rather, rock forcefully bombards them with messages of adult sexuality and even perversities, driving them into adult sexual experiences. This happens at the very age they have immature and developing concepts of love, commitment, and caring. According to Bloom, rock music in the American culture undermines parents' control over their children's moral education.[26]

Time has a great deal to do with rock music's powerful influence on our young people. The *Journal of the American Medical Association* has reported that "between the seventh and twelfth grades, the average teenager listens to 10,500 hours of rock music, just slightly less than the entire number of hours spent in the classroom from kindergarten through high school."[27]

Another study conducted by a professor of educational psychology revealed that heavy metal fans knew the lyrics of songs from memory more frequently than did general rock fans. Further, 41% of them claimed they knew the words to "all" their favorite songs as opposed to 25% of the general rock fans.[28] Another study revealed, "The finding that most adolescents report knowing many or all of the lyrics of their favorite songs is supported by Stipp [a researcher], who reported that all adolescents in his sample knew their favorite songs. A strikingly large number of the adolescents also said that they often agreed with the words."[29]

One student counselor who deals with adolescents often claims that he can detect rock music's influence on them. He has commented:

> The influence of rock music continued to surface in my counseling sessions with students. Time after time I saw them pattern their actions after the immoral behavior of their rock stars. The kids showed their allegiances by the vocabulary they picked up, by the song titles printed on their book jackets, by the posters they hung on the walls of their rooms at home, by the music they listened to in their cars, and by the clothes they wore.[30]

Even a police officer from Richmond, Indiana, complained, "Radio stations should refuse to play this kind of music. We get kids in the sheriff's office here all the time who mimic this behavior. I can tell this music has a negative influence on them."[31]

Al Menconi, a youth counselor who has specialized in rock music's influence on teenagers, has stated:

> The sad thing is that the majority of "Christian" kids I come in contact with have a stronger commitment to their music than to Jesus. Music is the language of today's generation.... I thought I understood peer pressure until I observed it first hand with my 12-year-old daughter, Ann. The pressure on her to conform to the Bon Jovi—Guns N' Roses—Bobby Brown—Madonna—George Michael lifestyles is unbelievable.... Every day kids identify who they are by their rock stars. Their heroes influence their values. And their values influence who they are. Today's young people don't listen to rock music, they experience it. It is their identity.[32]

All of this leads us to conclude that one of the pressing questions in regard to rock music is, "What are impressionable and vulnerable teens being taught concerning human sexuality, morality, Christianity, drug use, behavior toward others, the occult, and their philosophy of life in general?"

Whatever one may think about rock music, it cannot be denied that in some form, guidance and instruction are being given to young people. Rock videos, concerts, and magazines convey a powerful message, one that is too easily accepted and all too frequent. That message is revealed through rock's sounds and lyrics, and individual performers' lifestyles and worldviews.[33]

Consider MTV's "Rockumentary" series, which is devoted to interviews and documentaries of major rock groups. More than once it has revealed the destructive lifestyles of leading rock personalities—drugs, sex, alcohol, nihilism, hedonism, rebelliousness, lawlessness, and occultism. For example on August 3, 1991, members of Motley Crüe confessed some of the outrageous behavior that had become characteristic of their personal lives. Their existence had become so ravaged that the entire band could recognize the writing on the wall and see that their only choice was reform—either that or tragedy and even death.

The Dangerous Messages of Rock Music

In the material below we are going to illustrate the different messages modern rock and roll is conveying. But by what standard shall we measure these messages? If it is not an absolute standard, it doesn't count. If a standard is relative, it has nothing to say; every message is equally "moral." But God's standard, revealed in the Bible, is the absolute standard Christians must use to evaluate rock's messages.

In the pages to come we will briefly evaluate seven themes of modern rock music. The seven themes are: 1) the power of rock music to influence sexual behavior, 2) the power of rock music to influence violent behavior, 3) a comparison of the messages in rock and country music, 4) an examination of the "safe" rock groups—Hammer, Vanilla Ice, New Kids on the Block, 5) an examination of where rock is going in the future, 6) rock music's attack on Christian beliefs, and 7) rock and the occult.

(Again, this booklet can be used in conjunction with the video series, "Rock Music's Powerful Messages." The six programs correspond to the next six parts of this booklet [see note 3].)

2

Can Rock Music Influence Sexual Behavior?

Video Reference:
Rock Music's Powerful Messages,
Program One

Is it fair today to characterize rock music as conveying a message of sexual permissiveness? The answer is *yes*. According to *U.S. News and World Report*, March 19, 1990:

> Now there are at least 13 bands named after the male genitals, 6 after female genitals, 4 after sperm, 8 after abortion and one after a vaginal infection. A brief survey in *Maledicta* magazine by Purdue professors Joe Salmons and Monica Macauley (he plays in a regional rock band, Haunted Tank) also shows at least 10 bands named for various sex acts, 8 including the F-word, and 24 referring non-flatteringly to blacks, the disabled or homosexuals. Oddly, the authors could find no band named after excrement, but that was more than compensated for by the heavy emphasis on throwing up (6 bands, probably in admiration for the most famous of all rock Upchuckers, Johnny Vomit).

Today the different kinds of sexual behavior that are highlighted in modern rock music include premarital sex (fornication), adultery, sadomasochism, homosexuality, and even bestiality and necrophilia. Most frequently rock music simply calls its listeners to have sex with whomever they want to have sex. From the late Marvin Gaye's "Sexual Healing" to Queen's "Body Language" to George Michael's "I Want Your Sex" to Madonna's "Chemical Reaction" to White Snake's "Still Of the Night" and to the lyrics of Prince and endless others the theme is the same. The rock music videos of Robert Palmer ("Addicted to Love"), Rod Stewart ("Lost in You"), Bruce Springsteen ("I'm on Fire"), Cher ("Love and Understanding"), Madonna, and many others are frequently so brazen that the word indecency seems to have lost all meaning.

In spite of society's increased awareness of the rights of women, rock and roll frequently demeans women as sexual objects. More than one prominent rock star has boasted of literally thousands of sexual encounters with different women as if they were objects of conquest for his own pleasures, while in the next breath he turns around and refers to them as "sluts" and "prostitutes."

(CAUTION: The following material is sexually explicit. You may wish to pass over this material. The following are examples of how rock stars promote promiscuous sex through their music.)

In the song "Dungeon of Pleasure," the group Nasty Savage sings, "The bitch is bound and helpless, she is screaming for more. That sweet and innocent girl is really hard core. Her obsession with pain makes me bite my lip, as she eagerly indulges when I give her the whip."

In the song "Black and Blue," Van Halen leaves no doubt of what he is advocating: "Slip and slide, push it in. Bitch sure got the rhythm. I'm holding back, yea, I got control. Hooked into her system. Don't draw the line. Honey, I ain't through with you. The harder the better. Let's do it 'til we're black and blue."

In the song "Eat Me Alive" Judas Priest says, "Sounds like an animal panting to the beat. Groan in the pleasure zone, gasping from the heat; gut wrenching frenzy that destroys every joint, I'm gonna force you at gun point to eat me alive."

Similarly, many female rock stars feel no shame in promoting this same standard. For example, in Shenna Easton's "Sugar Walls" she says, "Blood races to your private spots. That lets me know there is a fire. You can't fight passion when passion is hot. Temperatures rise inside my sugar walls. Come spend the night inside my sugar walls. Heaven on earth inside my sugar walls."

Further, can anyone doubt that Madonna is actively promoting sexual promiscuity when she boasts, "I'm proud of my trashy image?"[34]

In our analysis we must consider the lifestyle of many rock stars. When Nikki Sixx of Motley Crüe was asked, What is the greatest reward of your success? He answered:

> The women. Damn, it seems like everywhere we go, there are thousands of girls just waiting to _____ us silly. I'm getting sick of all those sluts. What we like to do on the road is pick up a whole bus load of sluts and take them with us to the next town. We _____ their brains out and then pay for their

flights back home. Our manager hates us doing that; he says it costs too much money.[35]

Referring to their new release, Nikki said, "Our new album is raw, nasty, sleazy. I think it drips of sex."[36] According to *Rolling Stone*, September 4, 1980, a reporter for the magazine, commenting about his tour with Van Halen, observed, "I've seen enough naked women to fuel an article about porn rock." Van Halen's lastest album, "For Unlawful Carnal Knowledge," is anything but subtle, acronyms included.

In a 1991 concert at Madison Square Garden, Perry Farrell, lead singer for Jane's Addiction, said to the screaming audience, "Is everyone bored? Not now, I mean in your lives. Well if you really wanna _____ things up, go out and have a really good time. Stay alive and have really good sex. Just for me." In a spoken introduction to "Ain't No Right" he snapped, "My sex and my drugs are my _____ own business."[37] Two of the band members French-kissed.

But do these sexually explicit lyrics and statements by rock stars affect young people? The American Medical Association journal has revealed, "In a laboratory study of the effect of music television (MTV), Greeson and Williams found that 7th and 10th graders, after watching one hour of selected music videos, were more likely to approve of premarital sex compared with a controlled group of adolescents."[38]

Studies such as this may be why Allan Bloom writes that

> ... rock music has one appeal only, a barbaric appeal, to sexual desire—not love ... but sexual desire undeveloped and untutored.... Rock gives children, on a silver platter, with all the public authority of the entertainment industry, everything their parents always used to tell them they had to wait for until they grew up....
>
> Young people know that rock has the beat of sexual intercourse.... Never was there [such] an art form directed so exclusively to children.... The words implicitly and explicitly describe bodily acts that satisfy sexual desire and treat them as its only natural and routine culmination for children who do not yet have the slightest imagination of love, marriage or family. This has a much more powerful effect than does pornography on youngsters, who have no need to watch others do grossly what they can so easily do themselves. Voyeurism is for old perverts; active sexual

relations are for the young. All they need is encour-
agement.[39]

Compare the statements, actions, and lyrics of the above
rock artists with the biblical command in Ephesians 5:3
which says: "But among you there must not be even a hint of
sexual immorality, or of any kind of impurity, or of greed,
because these are improper for God's holy people."

The apostle Paul warns us, "Do not be deceived: Neither
the sexually immoral nor adulterers nor male prostitutes
nor homosexual offenders...will inherit the kingdom of
God" (1 Corinthians 6:9,10).

Then the Bible also tells us, "Flee from sexual immorality. All other sins a man commits are outside his body, but
he who sins sexually sins against his own body. Do you not
know that your body is a temple of the Holy Spirit...?"
(1 Corinthians 6:18,19).

Christians are further admonished: "For God did not call
us to be impure, but to live a holy life. Therefore, he who
rejects this instruction does not reject man but God, who
gives you his Holy Spirit" (1 Thessalonians 4:7).

THINGS TO THINK ABOUT[40]

1. Is it rational for non-Christians to unhesitatingly accept
   rock music's message of sexual permissiveness in light of
   the spread of AIDS (which will eventually kill tens of
   millions), and the transmission of 51 sexually transmitted diseases, many of which are now raging in society?
   Every nine months a new sexually transmitted disease
   is discovered; every year 12 million Americans contract a
   sexually transmitted disease—33,000 per day.[41]

2. MTV's "Rockumentary" on heavy metal music (noting
   that concerts are "seasoned with teen anger") cited
   leaders of various heavy metal bands and their fans. One
   fan observed that heavy metal "is more than music. It
   really is a lifestyle." The commentator noted it was a
   "celebration of sex, drugs and music that offers no apol-
   ogy." Ideas expressed by heavy metal stars or fans included the notion that concepts of sex, death, satanism
   and anything else necessary are used simply to outrage.
   One band member remarked, "We always write from the
   dark side of music.... We are not exactly waving the flag
   of goodness." What do you think is the root cause of
   heavy metal music?

3. An estimated 500 million (one-half *billion*) people in 26 countries viewed MTV's debut of the long version of Michael Jackson's sexually explicit and violence-laced video "Black or White"—tens of millions of them very young children who view Michael as a role model. This not only illustrates the power of rock music, it illustrates why the American Academy of Pediatrics urged parents to prevent their children from watching MTV because of its repeated themes of sex and violence. The AAP's policy statement reads: "Too many music videos promote sexism, violence, substance abuse, suicide and sexual behavior." Do you think you should discuss this subject with your children or parents? Why?

4. Scientists and musicologists agree that music can serve as a powerful encoder—that it can help order and give definition to our lives. Think of some examples of this in your own life or the life of someone close to you.

5. A Stanford University study found that music was the most common stimulus in evoking thrill-like responses in people (96% in fact, said they had experienced a "thrill" while listening to music). Can you think of a time when music has worked this particular magic on you? What particular emotion would you link with that thrill? Romantic love? Power? Religious awe? Lust? Rebellion?

6. Do the sexual messages conveyed by the rock stars we have cited conform to the scriptural standards given above?

7. How many secular rock groups can you name that uphold biblical standards concerning sexual behavior? How many can you name that don't? What does this tell you?

8. How would you characterize your present attitude concerning music?

9. Read Galatians 5:19,20 and note the 17 characteristics that mark the deeds of the flesh. Mentally examine your music collection and your favorite songs. Have any of the 17 characteristics found expression in your music? Of the characteristics that found expression in your music, identify those with which you have had a personal struggle. For example, if sexual lust is something you've heard about while listening to music and you have also personally engaged in it, acknowledge it. Be honest.

10. Apply Proverbs 4:20-27; Matthew 5:27-28; 15:8-20 and Luke 6:45 to your own habits of viewing rock videos.

3

Can Rock Music Influence Violent Behavior?

**Video Reference:
Rock Music's Powerful Messages,
Program Two**

The July 2, 1991, Guns N' Roses concert at St. Louis ended in a major riot involving 2,500 very angry fans and injuring over 60 people. *Rolling Stone* noted that "concert-goers went on a rampage, hurling bottles, destroying seats, pulverizing shrubbery, setting fires and laying waste to the band's equipment.... According to one fan, the carnage continued for an hour before officers in riot gear arrived and got the situation under control."[42] Unfortunately this is only one example of uncalled-for violence that has marred rock concerts—violence that has occasionally ended in death, for example at Altamont Race Track in 1969. Perhaps it isn't surprising.

Violence of many different types is increasingly found in modern rock music. In their song, "I Kill Children," the Dead Kennedys sing, "I kill children, I love to see them die. I kill children to make their mothers cry. I crush them under my car and I love to hear them scream. I feed them poison candy and spoil their Halloween. I kill children, I bang their heads in doors. I kill children, I can hardly wait for yours."

In the album "Hell Awaits" the band Slayer has the lyrics: "No apparent motive. Just kill and kill again. Survive my brutal slashing. I'll hunt you till the end."

The band Rigor Mortis in "Bodily Dismemberment" shouts: "There's no need to worry, bitch. Just lay there and relax. And as you reach your climax, I'll be reaching for my axe. With five easy slices, you're in six lovely pieces. Bodily dismemberment as passion increases."

Iron Maiden's mascot is "Eddy" a dead man who kills with great delight. According to Satanist and brutal murderer Richard Ramirez (the "Night Stalker"), it was AC/DC's song "Night Prowler" that became part of his motivation to murder 30 people. He said the song gave him "inspiration."[43] "Night Prowler" contains the stanza, "No one's gonna warn you, no one's gonna yell attack, and you can't feel the steel until it's hanging out your back, I'm your night prowler."

One survey revealed that among the favorite songs of 700 heavy metal fans 50% were about killing, 35.2% about satanism and 7.4% about suicide.[44] Sheila Davis, professor of lyric writing at New York University, comments that we "better give serious attention to the content of pop songs and to evaluate not only what lyrics are saying to society but, more importantly, what they may be doing to it."[45]

Similarly the National Council of Churches published a study asserting that we are the world's most violent nation and citing a "direct causal relationship between violence in the media and aggressive behavior in society."[46] *Time* magazine and national polls report that most Americans blame lyrics glorifying sex and violence for the increasing teen violence, noting that many people want more regulations of those lyrics. For example, according to Parents' Music Resource Center, a study of the Simons Market Research Bureau, released in 1986, indicated two-thirds of American adults are concerned that the lyrics in rock music are too sexually explicit, or glorify violence or the occult, and 75% agree that there should be a warning system while 80% want lyrics visible on the outside of the record jacket.[47] According to Dr. Paul King, assistant professor of child and adolescent psychiatry, "59.1% of the [adolescent] patients admitted primarily for chemical dependency made heavy metal their first choice of music. In addition, 74.4% were involved in violence, 49.8% in stealing, and 71.9% in sexual activity."[48]

Sadly, violence can also be directed inward and some rock musicians are conveying that message directly or indirectly. For example, Ozzy Osbourne's "Suicide Solution" advocates suicide ("Suicide is the only way out....").[49] In their song "Suicide's an Alternative" the band Suicidal Tendencies says, "Sick of life—it sucks / sick and tired—no one cares / sick of myself—don't wanna live / sick of living—gonna die / suicide's an alternative."

The band Metallica in their song "Fade to Black" says, "I have lost the will to live, simply nothing more to give; there is nothing more for me, need the end to set me free."

One study by educational psychologist Dr. Hannelore Wass, considered an expert on death and dying, indicated that while only 17% of the sample population of adolescents listened to music with blatantly destructive themes, the figure jumps to over 40% among juvenile delinquents.

Further, when asked whether rock songs about suicide or deadly violence could lead to suicide or murder with depressed or troubled youth, 40% of the general sample said yes, and 25% of heavy metal fans agreed. Typical comments were: "I've seen it happen to a classmate/friend, a song may push them over the edge"; "Hearing the thoughts out loud might push them to do it; songs put feelings in you"; "Songs and words are powerful; especially if it's a song by a band or singer they admire." Dr. Wass has concluded, "At this point in my research, I would say until we know for sure how this type of music can influence adolescents, it is vital for parents to monitor what their kids are listening to."[50]

Such studies have led the National Education Association to conclude that many of the 6,000 annual teen suicides may be linked to depression fueled by nihilistic and fatalistic lyrics.[51] Dr. Morton Kurland, a Palm Springs psychiatrist whose patient, John McCollum, committed suicide after listening to an Ozzy Osbourne record...[stated] "Sado-masochism, blood, and violence make big bucks for the producers of rock videos, but such things can push a [emotionally suffering] kid over the edge."[52] Unfortunately, millions of teenagers today are emotionally suffering.

Yet the themes of alienation, nihilism, and destruction that course through rock music are frequently only mirrors of the lives of rock musicians themselves. For example, the biography of Pink Floyd, *Saucerful of Secrets*, by the band's two former leaders gives vivid examples of the personal tragedy that can stalk the lives of those who glorify excess. (Cf. the 1991 Elton John interview with David Frost.)

Schwarz and Empey observe, "In talking with some of the musicians involved [in Satanism], as well as individuals they have consulted—researchers, psychologists, and psychics—a pattern becomes clear. Like so many others who have chosen Satanism over Christianity, they have a desire for immediate gratification and self-fulfillment. 'Money. Control. Power. They want the fantasy of being able to live a special life with a lot of wealth,' said one psychologist whose practice includes some of the major names in the rock business. 'And they're willing to die young to pay it off. They see that by giving up life early they can have everything....' The reality of this statement is obvious when you read the obituaries of rock stars. Many have died from alcoholism, drug abuse, or accidents resulting from their being under the influence of such products."[53]

Even the names of some of the bands in the heavy metal division termed "death metal" suggest a glorification of death and violence: "Blessed Death," "Carnivore," "Coroner," "Destruction," "Mace," "Malice," "Overkill," "Rotten Corpse," "Sacrifice," "Violence," etc.[54]

In his book *Heavy Metal Madness*, Dave Hart writes:

> Concerts feature skulls and skeletons, as well as simulated slashings, stabbings, and decapitations. Some even drink blood or gnaw on a few grisly bones. Some groups incorporate occult imagery, satanic rites or references to magic.... This is dark, angry music. It focuses on death and violence, and a love for blood and gore.... In many cases, the bands project a message that there can be no change, no hope, no future. All they can do is beat their fists in the empty air. Live fast and die young—go out in a blaze of glory.[55]

The *Journal of the American Medical Association (JAMA)* concluded:

> The violent and sexual content of the [rock] video images are disturbing to many. In one content analysis of 200 concept videos (distinguished from performance videos in which the predominant theme is a studio or concert performance), violence occurred in 57% of the samples and sexual imagery in 75%. Of the videos containing violence, 81% also contained sexual references. Half of all women who appeared in the videos were dressed provocatively. Another study showed that 59.7% of a random sample of rock had sexual themes, and 53.2% had violent themes.... Studies of the effects of television violence may also apply to music videos. These studies strongly suggest, but do not verify, that there is a causal connection between television violence and subsequent aggressive behavior. Gerbner and coworkers argue that television violence also may have a more subtle influence on social relationships.[56]

The *JAMA* article further noted that "several murders have been correlated with fascination for heavy metal music" and that "another behavioral study found that violent music videos desensitized viewers to violence immediately after viewing."[57] Additional research can be cited.[58]

The *JAMA* article expressed regret that the messages given to the youth by rock music are increasingly done "with disturbing lyrics that connote violence and pornographic sexual imagery."[59] Skid Row's album, "Slave to the

Grind," is characteristic with titles such as "Psycho-Love," "Riot Act," and "Get the _____ Out." "Riot Act" is an obligatory indictment of school as prison ("I didn't want your education 'cause it's nothing but a pile of _____"). Even *Rolling Stone* (Aug. 22, 1991) confessed the "vicious tenor" of "Get the _____ Out," describing it as "nothing more, or less, than gratuitous groupie bashing, a cheap macho swipe at a woman who is used, then abused just to satisfy...lust and ego."

Time magazine recently noted that "there is an acrid [bitter or caustic] tang in nearly every area of modern American pop culture" and that it is no longer possible to ignore what is happening.[60]

Compare rock's endorsement of violence with God's standards. The Bible teaches that we are not to glorify violence of any kind, whether it is suicide or sadomasochism. Rather, we are to live in peace and harmony with one another. We are admonished, "Let us therefore make every effort to do what leads to peace and mutual edification" (Romans 14:19). Jesus Himself taught, "Blessed are the peacemakers" (Matthew 5:9). We are told, "Turn from evil and do good; seek peace and pursue it" (Psalm 34:14).

God has called us to peace (1 Corinthians 7:15). God Himself is not a God of confusion, but of peace (1 Corinthians 14:33). The fruit of the Spirit is peace (Galatians 5:22) and we are to let the peace of Christ rule in our hearts (Colossians 3:15); we are to live in peace with one another (1 Thessalonians 5:13), and to pursue peace with all men (Hebrews 12:14).

On the other hand, "The Lord examines the righteous, but the wicked and *those who love violence*, his soul hates" (Psalm 11:5). "Do not envy a *violent* man or choose any of his ways, for the Lord detests a perverse man, but takes the upright into his confidence" (Proverbs 3:31,32). "Blessings crown the head of the righteous, but *violence* overwhelms the mouth of the wicked" (Proverbs 10:6). "A *violent* man entices his neighbor and leads him down a path that is not good" (Proverbs 16:29).

The apostle Paul admonishes us in Ephesians:

> Do not let any unwholesome talk come out of your mouths, but only what is helpful for building others up according to their needs, that it may benefit those who listen. And do not grieve the Holy Spirit of God, with whom you were sealed for the day of redemption. Get rid of all bitterness, rage and anger, brawling and slander, along with every form of malice. Be kind and

compassionate to one another, forgiving each other, just as in Christ God forgave you. Be imitators of God, therefore, as dearly loved children and live a life of love, just as Christ loved us and gave himself up for us" (Ephesians 4:29-32; 5:1,2).

The apostle further states that prayers and intercessions are to be made on behalf of everyone "that we may live peaceful and quiet lives in all godliness and holiness. This is good, and pleases God our Savior" (1 Timothy 2:1,2).

In conclusion, none can deny that the profanity, vulgarity, and violence in modern rock music violates the will of God for mankind.

THINGS TO THINK ABOUT

1. Do you think rock's message of violence, death, and suicide is needed to make the world a better place to live?

2. Realizing the power of music, what effect could the lyrics of a song advocating suicide have on a sensitive person who is depressed? Do you know people who seem to feed on such music? What can be done to help them?

3. According to 1 John 2:15-17, what does God say to a person who insists on loving the world's ways?

– 4 –

Drugs and Sexuality: Is There a Comparison Between the Messages in Rock and Country Music?

**Video Reference:
Rock Music's Powerful Messages,
Program Three**

No one can deny that there are messages in rock music encouraging drug use. In this section, we will compare the messages found in country with those in rock.

Rock Music and Drugs

As far back as 1969, *Time* magazine (September 26) commented, "Rock musicians use drugs frequently and openly and their compositions are riddled with references to drugs." Songs such as Velvet Underground's "Heroin" helped encourage some young people to experiment with drugs, not infrequently with tragic consequences.[61]

As reported in *Life* magazine, October 3, 1969, Jimi Hendrix, whose basic philosophy was one of unbridled sex and drug use, commented, "You can hypnotize people with music and when you get them at their weakest point, you can preach into the subconscious what *we* want to say."

But many famous rock stars have paid a price for their drug abuse. Among the dead are Brian Jones of the Rolling Stones, Sid Vicious of the Sex Pistols, Dennis Wilson of the Beach Boys, Jimi Hendrix, Jim Morrison of The Doors, Elvis Presley, Janice Joplin, Bon Scott of AC/DC, Frankie Lymon, Tim Harden, Phil Lynott of Thin Lizzie—and many others could be mentioned. The day this booklet was finished the lead singer for the Temptations, David Ruffin, died from a cocaine overdose. But in spite of this, drugs still play a prominent role in rock music and this seems to have a harmful effect on many who listen.

For example, one study in *Post Graduate Medicine* concluded that "evidence shows that such [rock] music promotes and supports patterns of drug abuse, promiscuous sexual activity and violence."[62]

The personal and social tragedy of modern drug abuse is simply unimaginable—and yet rock music continues to glorify drug use. In fact, it can be argued that rock music must assume a large share of responsibility for the modern drug epidemic. As in the area of human sexuality, rock musicians are failing to uphold their responsibilities. Steven Tyler of Aerosmith noted in *Sober Times* (Oct. 1988, p. 2) that "eight out of ten are using. It goes with the territory."

The Bible tells us we are to let nothing control us except the Holy Spirit of God. God desires that people be under His loving influence, rather than the influence of a drug substance that can harm them physically, socially, or spiritually. "Be very careful, then, how you live—not as unwise but as wise.... Do not get drunk on wine, which leads to debauchery. Instead, be filled with the Spirit" (Ephesians 5:15-18).

Further, the Bible tells us that we are to live "sensibly" in the world. How can a person justify the use of heroin, cocaine, LSD and other psychedelics, or marijuana, or the abuse of alcohol, amphetamines, and depressants and believe he is living sensibly?

> Be hospitable, loving what is good, sensible, just, devout, self-controlled.... Older men are to be temperate, dignified, sensible, sound in faith, in love, in perseverance...instructing us to deny ungodliness and worldly desire and to live sensibly, righteously and godly in the present age. This is a trustworthy statement; and concerning these things I want you to speak confidently, so that those who have believed God may be careful to engage in good deeds. These things are good and profitable for men (Titus 1:8; 2:2,12;3:8 NASB).

The Bible asks "Do you not know that your body is a temple of the Holy Spirit, who is in you, whom you have received from God? You are not your own; you were bought with a price. Therefore, honor God with your body" (1 Corinthians 6:19,20). God encourages us to care for our body (Ephesians 5:28-30). These Scriptures are incompatible with drug use which is illegal and harmful.

Now let's examine some of the messages in country music.

Country Music's Messages

Country and Western is a uniquely American institution whose musical style and honesty of expression have endeared it to millions who empathize with its realistic portrayal of the ups and downs of life.

Country music is a different genre of music than rock and is usually associated with motherhood, home, the flag, and apple pie. Nevertheless, its ethics in the areas of substance abuse, treatment of women, sexual morality, and even occultism,[63] are in some cases similar to those in rock music. When country music degrades womanhood and glorifies drunkenness, drugs, premarital sex, and adultery, it contributes to the undermining of American society as thoroughly as rock music. Despite the more "wholesome" appearance, when country music adopts such themes, it erodes family and social stability.

According to *People* magazine, Conway Twitty, perhaps the most popular country artist of all time, reflected on his career by confessing, "As a country artist, I'm not proud of a lot of things in my field. There is no doubt in my mind that we are contributing to the moral decline in America."[64]

Would you agree that the following song titles characterize an attitude of sexual permissiveness?—"To All the Girls

I've Loved Before," "I Cheated on a Good Woman's Love," "I'd Love to Lay You Down," "I Just Can't Stay Married to You," "Now I Lay Me Down to Cheat."

Substance abuse is also a problem in country music. *Billboard* magazine (October 11, 1980) noted that "drugs are turning up in country songs with surprising frequency, along with frank references to sex." Jimmy Buffet's "Why Don't We Get Drunk" (containing the stanza, "Why don't we get drunk and screw?"); Willie Nelson's "I Gotta Get Drunk" ("I gotta get drunk, I can't stay sober"); and other songs like "Bombed, Boozed, and Busted," "Caffeine, Nicotine, Benzedrine, and Wish Me Luck," "Quaaludes Again" and "Drinkin', Druggin', and Watchin' TV" all reveal that many country songs are promoting substance abuse.

Here is what one noted researcher concluded about the effects of the messages found in country music:

> Dr. James Scheafer, Ph.D., Director of the University of Minnesota's office of alcohol and other drug abuse programming, has discovered that country music can lead to alcoholism among listeners.... There is definitely a correlation between high-risk country and western songs and drinking, especially those of Kenny Rogers, Waylon Jennings, and Hank Williams.... A recent press release about Johnny Paycheck's upcoming album had this to say: "Yes, I do cocaine, but cocaine isn't a killer drug and neither is alcohol. Heroin is a problem and P.C.P. is a killer drug. Cocaine and Alcohol are OK upfront drugs."[65]

Country music is a one-half billion dollar a year industry boasting 2,500 country music stations with tens of millions of fans. Unfortunately, books like *Nashville Babylon: The Uncensored Truth and Private Lives of Country Music's Greatest Stars* seem to indicate the death and tragedy rate among country music stars is as bad as that in rock music. Perhaps the somewhat melancholic emphasis of country music—depression, broken lives and relationships, alienation, adultery, and the downside of life—coupled with the increase in use of drugs, sex, and drinking can become a kind of self-fulfilling prophecy for some people. But there is no reason why country music can't emphasize the positive side to life and truly honor relationships, clean living, marriage, and spirituality. It increasingly is! Don Williams and many other country musicians have combined recognition of the pain of life with a positive message as well.

Nevertheless, even though country music has a more wholesome image than rock music does—if both are conveying antibiblical standards then Christians are commanded to reject such standards.

The Bible instructs us to:

> Behave decently, as in the daytime, not in orgies and drunkenness, not in sexual immorality and debauchery, not in dissension and jealousy. Rather, clothe yourselves with the Lord Jesus Christ, and do not think about how to gratify the desires of the sinful nature (Romans 13:13,14).

> Marriage should be honored by all, and the marriage bed kept pure, for God will judge the adulterer and all the sexually immoral (Hebrews 13:4).

THINGS TO THINK ABOUT

1. John Cale, recalling his days in the Velvet Underground illustrated their philosophy with "Give people hard drugs. Give them the drugs they want. Acid? Give 'em heroin" (*Spin*, May 1990, p. 30). Even with society waging a "war on drugs" and many rock stars dead from overdose, why do you think most rock stars continue to use drugs?

2. Country and western music often has a "cleaner, healthier" image than rock. Do you think this image is justified? Why?

3. The tragic lives of a large number of country and western stars have been revealed in many bestselling books. Why do you think so many country music stars write songs that reflect themes of drinking, sex, marital infidelity, divorce, frustration, and despair?

4. If art reflects culture, what does rock and country music say about American culture?

5. Has country music given in to degrading practices in our culture, or helped cause them? Why?

6. Many country stars have a desire to promote family values and patriotism, yet their lyrics may work against them. Why do you think this irony exists?

What About the "Safe" Rock Groups—Hammer, Vanilla Ice, New Kids on the Block?

**Video Reference:
Rock Music's Powerful Messages,
Program Four**

What about the so-called safe rock groups—Hammer, Vanilla Ice, New Kids on the Block, and others? While their rejection of the drug culture is commendable, they often retain a sensuous or hedonistic philosophy with similarities to rock. These groups are supposed to be good, clean-cut entertainers, but can their standards be successfully defended when compared with biblical standards? They are making a laudable effort to improve the image of contemporary rock music; nevertheless, there are other messages being conveyed besides that of "say no to drugs."

Hammer is a gifted artist and dancer with a strong church background who says he once considered going into the ministry. But the message being conveyed in some of his videos is not that sexual promiscuity is wrong; it is only wrong when you are not "old enough" to do it.

Vanilla Ice is also against drug use. He doesn't use vulgar language (on stage) and is a more respectable performer than many. Nevertheless, sexual innuendos remain. The standard of sexuality is simply not the biblical standard that Christian young people should follow.

The New Kids on the Block have the clean-cut look. They don't use drugs, but they, too, have a different sexual standard than God has given. Many Christian mothers accompany their kids to see their shows, at which thousands of preteenage girls become emotionally swept away, squealing and screaming at the sexual gyrations and innuendos of the band. Do Christian mothers think that such behavior is godly?

We question the kind of messages being conveyed by these "safe" groups. The Bible says, "But among you there must not even be a *hint* of sexual immorality, or of any kind of impurity..." (Ephesians 5:3).

All Christians are to ask what kind of impact these cleaner groups are having on impressionable preteen and teenage youth. What are such groups telling young people about their sexuality? Are they being indoctrinated to the world's philosophy of sex? Are the sexual innuendos being conveyed by these groups helping them to say no to a sexually permissive culture? Or do these groups break down the resistance of young people to Christian teaching on morality? With AIDS and 51 other sexually transmitted diseases making the rounds, do you think the "safe rock" groups are being as socially responsible as they should?

To answer these important questions, we turn to Eric Holmberg's evaluation of New Kids on the Block.

What About the New Kids on the Block?[*]

New Kids on the Block (NKOTB) is a very popular group of five young male singers who were intentionally developed and positioned by their management as a "safe" band—an alternative to the blatant excesses of regular rock and roll. They rail against drugs, profess a belief in God, sing about love, and live with their folks.

What could be wrong with NKOTB? Well, we might ask their founder, song writer, and guiding light, producer—impresario Maurice Starr. As he told one newspaper reporter, "I'm going to get out of this....I'll go perform gospel music. I've got to save my soul and those of others. That's going to be where I take my stand and when I'm in that field, I don't want to be in this one anymore."[66] Why does he need to get away from the New Kids scene before he can save his and other people's souls? Could it be that when you cut through the thin veneer of the marketing hype that surrounds these guys, you find the same tired formula that has made every rock n' roll star—sex, fantasy, and emotional seduction? Too harsh? Consider this:

1. *Spin* magazine observed the following: "The moves, with the exception of Joey (whose explicit gyrations suggest that he is either taking serious advantage of his sex symbol status or is simply too naive to question his choreographer), consist of standard showbiz spins...."[67] *Time* magazine described their concert: "It's as if the concert stage were a reef in some Sargasso Sea of raging teenage hormones."[68]

---

[*] From *Hell's Bells*, by Eric Holmberg (revised and used by permission).

2. A Christian writer reviewed their concert special on the Disney Channel: "The most disturbing moment came during a song called 'She's My Cover Girl,' which starts out: 'I get up in the morning and I see your face / You're looking so good, everything's in place / Don't you know I could never make you sigh / Won't you stay here with me and be my bride?' (Just a hint, he's sleeping with her, but they're not married yet.) During this sexual innuendo, a little girl (who appeared to be only about six years old) gave the singer a rose. It was a tender moment, quickly marred by a shift on the other side of the stage where the singer proclaimed, 'I only wanna be with you—like this...!' with two sharply pronounced pelvic thrusts. The girls screamed. The Kids all wagged their behinds at the teen and preteen audience. The girls screamed again. The singer stripped off his T-shirt. And the girls screamed some more."[69]

3. Donnie Wahlberg, the unofficial leader of the group, appears on the August 13 issue of *People* magazine wearing a nose ring, a scowl, and a skull and crossbones on his jacket. On their popular "Step by Step" video as well as during his guest V.J. stint on MTV he conspicuously wore a Public Enemy T-shirt. Public Enemy is a rap group noted for its advocacy of Louis Farrakhan and the militant, racist Black Muslim religion. According to the *New York Times* (March 28, 1991) Wahlberg surrendered to police after a warrant was issued for his arrest on a charge of arson. *People Weekly* (Sept. 24, 1991) reported on his assault against airline passenger Benjamin Dattner, noting that New Kids Joe McIntyre and Jonathan Knight have also been involved in physical assaults against others. Perhaps such incidents should make us wonder if NKOTB is the exemplary Christian band that thousands of young girls say it is.

Are NKOTB concerts conducive to a close walk with Jesus Christ? Are parents so naive as to think that it's fine for a singer to suggestively thrust his pelvis at their screaming daughters? Or does believing in the "Almighty Creator" and being cute make that all right?[70] Can we encourage our teenage and even preteen daughters to become boy crazy, turn them loose in a world so charged with unrestrained sexual energy that it's ready to explode, and then expect to see them remain virgins? Today, five or six out of ten girls will be sexually active by the time they're finished with high school. Should we be surprised?

Things to Think About

1. Rock historians, Seay and Neely, comment in their *Stairway to Heaven*: "Rock 'n Roll, the most powerful music the world has ever known, has a lot to answer for...crimes against art and humanity, the spirit and itself. But for those who love the music...the power of rock is kind of a religious mystery itself. It makes people feel really bad and really good. It brings out some of our noblest and most of our meanest impulses....In some way that's both wonderful and awful, we receive blessings and curses." Evaluate this comment and apply it to the "safe rock" groups.

2. In *The Secret Power of Music*, David Tame argues: "Surely the lowest common denominator which determines the precise nature of any musical work is the mental and emotional state of the composer and/or performer. It is the essence of this state which enters into us, tending to mold and shape our own consciousness into conformity with itself. Through music portions of the consciousness of the musician become assimilated by the audience."[71] Do you agree with this assessment? How could it apply to "safe rock"?

3. Should parents encourage their children to listen to "safe rock" groups who advocate abstaining from drugs if those same groups break God's standards of sexual purity? In an era where sex increasingly maims and kills could "clean" rock or "safe" rock be a contradiction in terms? (Cf. 1 John 1:5-7, 2:4-6,15-17; Rom. 13:14; 2 Tim. 2:22; Col. 2:8-10.)

6

Where Is Rock Music Headed?

**Video Reference:
Rock Music's Powerful Messages,
Program Five**

Certain groups are currently on the cutting edge of rock music. They are not considered mainline bands, but may indicate where rock music or portions of it are headed. Why? Because many mainline groups look to them for new ideas.

We turn to three new rock groups that will show us where rock may be heading. They are: Jane's Addiction, Gwar, and Glen Danzig.[72]

What can we expect to see in the future? Jane's Addiction is an anarchistic band whose cacophonous music has contorted heavy metal into an even more complex and depressing sound. Replete with stage shows displaying icons of Santernian [e.g. witchcraft] magic, the band has "admitted a dalliance with needles and hard drugs." Both their work and concerts (for example, the bestselling album "Nothings Shocking") are reminiscent of the Sex Pistols earlier proclamation, "We're not into music; we're into chaos." *Details for Men* magazine's special music issue (July 1991) described a Jane's Addiction concert at Madison Square Garden. Amidst a stage "draped with Santernian magic icons . . . the Garden is a mass of wretched adolescence: metal kids, hip-hoppers, [Grateful] Deadheads and death rockers, slam dancing in the aisles, pissing between the seats. They've come to see outlaw charisma. . . ." Lead singer Perry Farrell argues, "You don't have a society until the society is completely shameless" and that "drugs can be beneficial and they are necessary."[73]

Spin magazine describes Gwar's concerts today with these words: "The Gwar live show is like KISS in Sensurround. . . . In concert, one can expect to see: Oderous' brain explode; Sexecutioner (do unmentionable), and various liquids (blood of slaves, semen, brain, puke, etc.) spewed into the crowd."[74]

For example, while on stage, band members of Gwar cut off a mock human head and simulated blood spurts out over the audience. Band members take the blood and wipe it on their faces and over their bodies and even drink it. They bring out an animal on stage and disembowel it. They smear its blood over their bodies and take the animal's entrails and wrap them around their necks.

Elton John once commented that all kinds of sexual freedom should be permitted and encouraged, but "I draw the line at goats." Perhaps Gwar doesn't; they simulate having sex with a goat on stage.

Spin magazine has proclaimed Glen Danzig to be one of the most up-and-coming new rock stars. Yet Danzig promises to shock those who think they have seen it all and are unshockable.

According to *Spin* (Jan. 1991, p. 29) Danzig "embodies both rock's past glories and the promise of its future." Yet in songs like "Am I Demon," "Mother," and others, he glorifies occult ritual and sacrifice, violence and spiritual anarchy. In one blasphemous video a woman at the foot of the cross looks up and sees not Jesus but a graphic portrayal of the devil—arms outstretched—hanging on the cross. The immediate impression this powerful image gives is either that Jesus was really the devil or that what the cross symbolizes is satanic.

In light of all this, the apostle Paul seemed to be writing of rock when he said:

> There will be terrible times in the last days. People will be lovers of themselves, lovers of money, boastful, proud, abusive, disobedient to their parents, ungrateful, unholy, without love, unforgiving, slanderous, without self-control, brutal, not lovers of the good, treacherous, rash, conceited, lovers of pleasure rather than lovers of God—having a form of godliness but denying its power. Have nothing to do with them. They are the kind who worm their way into homes and gain control over weak-willed women, who are loaded down with sins and are swayed by all kinds of evil desires (2 Timothy 3:1-6).

In many of these new groups, rebellion against the establishment's traditional values and Christian morality is advocated. But how much more rebellious can future rock musicians become?

Historically, rebellion has been as much a part of rock and roll as sex or drugs. From its inception, rock music has promoted rebellion against both parents and society.

In an early interview in *Rolling Stone* magazine, David Crosby of Crosby, Stills, & Nash commented, "I figured the only thing to do was to swipe their kids. . . . By saying that, I'm not talking about kidnapping. I'm just talking about changing their value systems, which removes them from their parents' world very effectively."[75]

Paul Kanter of Jefferson Starship confesses: "Our music is intended to broaden the generation gap, to alienate children from their parents. . . ."[76]

Mick Jagger of the Rolling Stones has remarked, "There is no such thing as a secure, family-oriented rock and roll song."[77]

Jon of Bon Jovi observed, "I wanted to rebel against anything and everything, and it happened that I was able to do it by playing rock and roll in a band."[78]

John Cougar reveals, "I swear or cuss because I know that it's not socially acceptable. I hate things that are 'this is the way you are supposed to behave.' That is why I hate schools, governments, and churches."[79]

Nikki Sixx of Motley Crüe comments:

> We never set out to be anybody's role model. But since we have become that, we are trying to give our fans something to believe in. On the second album, we told them to "Shout at the Devil." A lot of people . . . think that song is about Satan. That's not true. It's about standing up to authority, whether it is your parents, your teacher or your boss. That is pretty good advice, I think. But I'm sure that any parent who hears it is going to think it is treason.[80]

Gene Simmons of KISS says, "Survival's gotta do with believing in yourself. People are going to tell you that you can't do this. They can all go _____ themselves collectively. You know, you don't need those people around, and that includes your parents. If people aren't supporting you, then they are your enemies. Get rid of those leeches and go after your dreams."[81]

But such statements are diametrically opposed to what God says in the Bible. The fifth commandment teaches, "Honor your father and your mother. . ." (Exodus 20:12). The New Testament teaches, "Children, obey your parents in the Lord, for this is right. 'Honor your father and mother'— which is the first commandment with a promise—'that it may go well with you and that you may enjoy long life on the earth'" (Ephesians 6:1-3).

In addition, the Bible teaches that we are not to rebel

against society or government or those in authority. "Everyone must submit himself to the government authorities, for there is no authority except that which God has established. The authorities that exist have been established by God. Consequently, he who rebels against the authority is rebelling against what God has instituted and those who do so will bring judgment on themselves" (Romans 13:1,2).

In another passage we read, "Remind the people to be subject to rulers and authorities, to be obedient, to be ready to do whatever is good, to slander no one, to be peaceable and considerate, and to show true humility toward all men" (Titus 3:1,2).

When rock music in general promotes rebellion against parents and society, it opposes the teachings of God in His Word: "For rebellion is as the sin of witchcraft" (1 Sam. 15:23).

Finally, rock is increasingly turning to the occult, suggesting the future may see more promotion of altered states of consciousness, spirit contact, and other occult practices through music (see Chapter 8).

THINGS TO THINK ABOUT

1. Where do you think rock is headed in the future and why? Consider the following argument: "Music will continue to evolve and reflect and change its culture. As the culture goes, so goes the music. We have already gone from 'wine, women and song' to 'drugs, sex and rock and roll.'" If this is true, where do you think rock is headed in the future? Jim Morrison said, "I am interested in anything about revolt, disorder, chaos. . . ." Apply Rom. 13:1,2.

2. Sociologist Allan Bloom comments, "The result [of the influence of rock] is nothing less than parents' loss of control over their children's moral education at a time when no one else is seriously concerned with it."[82] Do you think this is true? Why? What are the implications?

3. "Rock is very big business, bigger than the movies, bigger than professional sports, bigger than television, and this accounts for much of the respectability of the music business."[83] Should money and wealth determine respectability? Or be envied? (Discuss Prov. 11:28; 28:6,20; Matt. 19:23; Lk. 6:24; 12:21; 2 Cor. 6:10; Ja. 2:5-7; 5:1-3.)

4. Do you think future generations will look back with respect and admiration on today's rock music? Why?

7

How Does Rock Music Reject Christian Beliefs?

Video Reference:
Rock Music's Powerful Messages,
Program Six

Rock music almost unanimously rejects Christian standards and beliefs. For example, reading through a text like *Rock and Roll Babylon* is as depressing as reading *Hollywood Babylon*; the antiChristian nature of these subcultures are laid bare in graphic terms. From The Doors' Jim Morrison's mocking, screaming hatred of Christian prayer ("Petition the Lord with Prayer") to Skid Row's "Quicksand Jesus" ("Are we saved by the words of bastard saints?") to the more explicit blasphemies, rock culture has often identified its aversion to Christian faith. Another example of this is "The Oath" by the band King Diamond: "I deny Jesus Christ, the deceiver, and I adjure the Christian faith, holding in contempt all of its works."

Another example is "Possessed" by the band Venom which says, "I am possessed by all that is evil. The death of your God I demand. I . . . sit at Lord Satan's right hand," and "I drink the vomit of the priest, make love to the dying whore, Satan is my master incarnate, hail, praise to my unholy host."

Billy Idol attempts "to show what a human rip-off religion is."[84] Leon Russell thinks that "organized Christianity has done more harm than any other single force I can think of in the world" and suggests that the religion of rock and roll replace it.[85] In an interview in *Spin*, Sinéad O'Connor emphasized, "It's a huge abuse to teach children that God is not within themselves. *That* God is pollution. That God is bigger than them. That God is outside them. That is a lie. That's what causes the emptiness of children."[86]

In "Hymn 43" the band Jethro Tull conveyed this message, "We are our own saviors, and if Jesus saves, then He better save Himself." Ozzy Osbourne says, "I'm not a born-again Christian. I'm a born-again Hitler."[87]

In 1966, John Lennon boasted that Christianity would pass away and that the Beatles were more popular than Jesus. In his book *A Spaniard in the Works*, he portrayed

Christ under the guise of a character he named "Jesus L. Pifco, a garlic eating, stinking, little yellow greasy fascist bastard Catholic Spaniard."[88]

Is it really surprising that rock music, which often incorporates drugs, sex, nihilism, amoralism, and rebellion into its lyrics, would also openly oppose God, His Son, and the gospel? But at what price? Consider the following.

We can never get rid of Jesus Christ. Jesus is a real person who lived in history, was crucified, and rose from the dead. Jesus made the astonishing claim that He was God in human flesh.*

Jesus also said that each of us would finally be accountable to Him alone and that He will hold us responsible for what we did with the life He gave us. Specifically, did we believe on Him, receive Him by faith—did we obey or disobey Him by our choices and our actions?

According to Jesus, every person who has ever lived will have to stand before Him at the end of time and give an account of his life. "Moreover, the Father judges no one, but has entrusted all judgment to the Son" (John 5:22). And "When the Son of Man comes in his glory, and all the angels with him, he will sit on his throne in heavenly glory. All the nations will be gathered before him, and he will separate the people one from another as a shepherd separates the sheep from the goats. He will put the sheep on his right and the goats on his left. . . . Then they will go away to eternal punishment, but the righteous to eternal life" (Matthew 25:31-33,46).

Did you know that your eternal destiny depends on what you do with Jesus Christ? Jesus matters. He won't be ignored. Perhaps you are someone who wonders what Jesus can do for you? Jesus says that He alone can give you peace and joy that you can't find in life without Him. When a person receives Jesus Christ as his personal Savior, the Holy Spirit changes that person's inner desires. As a result, his outward behavior begins to change. The difference between the lifestyle promoted by our sinful nature and that brought by the Spirit of God can be seen in this biblical passage:

> The acts of the sinful nature are obvious: sexual immorality, impurity and debauchery; idolatry and witchcraft; hatred, discord, jealousy, fits of rage, selfish

---

* See our *The Case for Jesus the Messiah* (Harvest House) and *Do the Resurrection Accounts Conflict? and What Proof Is There Jesus Rose from the Dead?* (Ankerberg Theological Research Institute).

ambition, dissensions, factions and envy; drunkenness, orgies, and the like. I warn you, as I did before, that those who live like this will not inherit the kingdom of God. But the fruit of the Spirit is love, joy, peace, patience, kindness, goodness, faithfulness, gentleness and self-control. Against such things there is no law (Galatians 5:19-23).

The Bible says, "For all [of us] have sinned and fall short of the glory of God" (Romans 3:23). Jesus came to earth and died on the cross paying the penalty for sin that was due to each of us. First Peter 3:18 says, "For Christ died for sins once for all, the righteous for the unrighteous, to bring you to God." Do you desire to receive Jesus Christ as your personal Lord and Savior? If so, acknowledge your sin before God and be willing to turn from it. Tell Jesus you are changing your mind about Him and your sin and receive Him. If you desire to have Christ change you and forgive you of your past right now, you may pray this prayer:

> Dear God. I admit that I am a sinner. I believe that Jesus Christ died on the cross to forgive my sins. I now place my faith in Him as my Lord and Savior. I know there are things in my life that have been displeasing to you. I ask you to forgive me and help me to live a life that is pleasing to you. I thank you that you have taken all of my sins away and have given me eternal life. Amen.

If you prayed that prayer, please write us at The John Ankerberg Show for some helpful materials on growing in the Christian life. It is important that you attend a church where the Bible is honored and Christ is accepted as Lord, that you read the Bible, beginning with the New Testament and Psalms and Proverbs, and that you talk to God daily in prayer. These things will help you to grow in your new relationship with Christ. "Now, therefore, fear the Lord and serve him in sincerity and truth, and put away the (false) gods...choose for yourselves today whom you will serve" (Joshua 24:14,15).

THINGS TO THINK ABOUT

1. In *The Real Frank Zappa Book* (1989, p. 259), Frank Zappa said, "My best advice to anyone who wants to raise a happy, mentally healthy child is: Keep him or her as far away from a church as you can."

   If a person listens to and watches the images and messages of rock music 25 to 35 hours a week, while only devoting one hour a week to the teachings of God's Word, which philosophy will have the most influence on him? Which will that person eventually adopt? Which will eventually mold his choices? Which will he learn to love and imitate? To again bring this down to a personal level, to which philosophy are you exposing yourself now?

2. In God's Word we are told not to conform ourselves to the values and philosophy of this world. "Do not conform any longer to the pattern of this world, but be transformed by the renewing of your mind" (Romans 12:2). In Proverbs we are told that above all else, we should guard our heart, for out of it come the issues of life (Proverbs 4:23). We are told to let no evil thing come before our eyes (Psalm 101:3). Rather, "Whatever is true, whatever is noble, whatever is right, whatever is pure, whatever is lovely, whatever is admirable ... think about such things" (Philippians 4:8). We are further told, "Set your mind on things above, not on earthly things" (Colossians 3:1,2). In light of these and many other Scriptures, how can a Christian be immersed in modern rock music, looking at the powerful images and messages it conveys, day in and day out, and not think that he is offending and disobeying his Lord?

3. A "Slayer" fan commented, "I hate your God, Jesus Christ. Satan is my lord. I sacrifice animals for him. My god is Slayer. Its the words of their music I believe in" (*Spin*, May 1989, p. 94). If you are a non-Christian, rock music may be conveying exactly what you want, including sex, drugs, experimenting with the occult, and the freedom to rebel. But keep in mind, the kinds of attitudes and behaviors advocated through rock music have resulted in destroying more lives than can be mentioned. Think of how many people have been initiated into drug use because rock music has glamorized that behavior? How many people have picked up a sexually transmitted disease as a result of living out rock music's message concerning sexual promiscuity? Probably millions.

No one should be deceived—the values one adopts will either bless his life or curse it. The Bible says, "Do not be deceived: God cannot be mocked. A man reaps what he sows. The one who sows to please his sinful nature, from that nature will reap destruction; the one who sows to please the Spirit, from the Spirit will reap eternal life" (Galatians 6:7,8). Can anyone logically deny that the lifestyle promoted in rock is frequently, socially and personally destructive? Then why do you think it is so popular?

8

Does Rock Music Support the Occult?

Video Reference:
The Dangers of Rock Music,
Series Two, Program One

The text *Unfinished Symphonies: Voices From the Beyond* by medium Rosemary Brown is a book describing how she receives communications from the spirit world. She communicates regularly with the alleged dead, in this case, supposedly, the great composers of the past—Chopin, Mozart, Bach, Liszt, Debussy, Rachmaninoff, Brahms, Shumann, etc. These spirits talk to Ms. Brown, visit her regularly, and possess her, guiding her hands to both play and write, in manuscript form, music that is far beyond her own abilities. Ms. Brown has been investigated by numerous musical experts, interviewed by Leonard Bernstein, and has been the subject of many investigative reports without fraud being detected. She claims that these spirits have possessed her in order to communicate both their music and their message from beyond. Through her, the spirits compose in styles quite similar, if not identical, to the ancient dead composers. She has released several albums of her music including a new Brahms' string quartet.

But we think the evidence reveals that these entities are not the dead but rather are lying spirits which the Bible identifies as demons. We have cited persuasive reasons for this conclusion in our book *Cult Watch: What You Need to Know About Spiritual Deception*, Parts 5 and 7.

Why would demons impersonate the spirits of dead composers and give musical compositions through an earthly medium? It seems their primary reason is to use the phenomenon as a vehicle with which to dispense occultic philosophy. Rosemary Brown was an accomplished medium before she encountered the spirits claiming they were the great composers. She says, "The first time I saw Franz Liszt, I was about seven years old, and already accustomed to seeing the spirits of the so-called dead" (p. 9).

Nevertheless, these supposedly refined spirits of dead composers actively promote the same old paganism and mediumistic philosophy found among occultists of all stripes.

There is no reason to fear death because everyone allegedly experiences reincarnation (pp. 110-114). The spirits teach pantheism and encourage the development of psychic abilities (pp. 114-123). They deny and reject biblical teaching. Consider one of the alleged statements of "Liszt" in response to Brown:

> I remarked that because of the usual Christian beliefs there are people who believe that one has to be "saved" here on earth. "That is not true," he said. "When people die...they still have the chance to go on and to catch up [after death]" (p. 110).

In other words, these lying spirits will use the medium of music to further their own purposes—to deceive men and women concerning biblical teaching (e.g., Hebrews 9:27; Genesis 1:1). The Rosemary Brown phenomenon and her spirit guides also encourage the practice of necromancy (communication with the alleged dead), something the Bible clearly forbids (Deuteronomy 18:9-12).

Consider another illustration. Cyril Scott was an eminent composer during his lifetime. He was a student of the occult religion known as Theosophy and also interested in the occultic potential of music. Two of his books, *The Influence of Music on History and Morals* and *Music: Its Secret Influence Throughout the Ages*, were received through inspiration of the spirit world by one of the Theosophic spirit guides that influenced the founder of Theosophy, Madame Blavatsky. In the latter book, Scott tells us that from his talks with this spirit it:

> ...takes a special interest in the evolution of Western music....Indeed, he considers it advisable that students of occultism of all schools should more fully appreciate the great importance of music as a force in spiritual [occult] evolution, and to this end he has revealed much that has hitherto not been revealed, and that cannot fail to prove of paramount interest to all music-lovers (p. 32).

Scott himself is convinced that "the great Initiates [in the spirit world] have vast and imposing plans for the musical future" (p. 199). What is this plan? It is to use music as an occult medium through which to develop altered states of consciousness, psychic abilities, and contact with the spirit world. Scott explains:

Music in the future is to be used to bring people into yet closer touch with the Devas [spirits]; they will be enabled to partake of the benefic [beneficial] influence of these beings while attending concerts at which by the appropriate type of sound they have been invoked.... The scientifically calculated music in question, however, will achieve the two-fold object of invoking the Devas and at the same time stimulating in the listeners those [psychic] faculties by means of which they will become aware of them and responsive to their [the spirits'] influence (pp. 200,201).

Scott concludes his book by citing the words of his spirit guide: "Today, as we enter this new Age, we seek, primarily through the medium of *inspired music*, to defuse the spirit of [occultic] unification and brotherhood, and thus quicken the [spiritual] vibration of this planet" (p. 204). This genre of "inspired music" is now found in local record stores. Some "New Age" music is spiritistically inspired for specific occult goals. The "composers" of the New Age music claim it can foster meditation, help develop psychic power, alter consciousness, induce "astral" travel, and transform personality. Other contemporary rock musicians parallel these ideas.

Many of the big-time rock stars have been heavily involved not only in the occult but also in overt Satanism.... Trying to describe his own "inspiration" process, [John] Lennon said: "It's like being possessed: like a psychic or a medium."... Of the Beatles, Yoko Ono has said, "They were like mediums. They weren't conscious of all they were saying, but it was coming through them."... Marc Storace, vocalist with the heavy-metal band Krokus, told *Circus* magazine: "You can't describe it except to say it's like a mysterious energy that comes from the metaphysical plane and into my body. It's almost like being a medium."... "Little Richard" had similar experiences and identified Satan as the source of his inspiration: "I was directed and commanded by another power. The power of darkness... that a lot of people don't believe exists. The power of the devil. Satan." Jim Morrison [of The Doors] called the spirits that at times possessed him "the Lords," and wrote a book of poetry about them. Folk rock artist Joni Mitchell's creativity came from her spirit guide "Art." So dependent was she upon "Art" that nothing could detain her when he "called."

The prevalence of such "spirits" among top rock stars seems to go beyond the realm of coincidence. Superstar Jimi Hendrix, called "rock's greatest guitarist" ... "believed he was possessed by some spirit," according to Alan Douglas. Hendrix's former girlfriend, Fayne Pridgon, has said: "He used to always talk about some devil or something was in him, you know, and he didn't have any control over it, he didn't know what made him act the way he acted and what made him say the things he said, and songs ... just came out of him...."[89]

In the early years, Rolling Stones' Mick Jagger and Keith Richards were friendly with underground filmmaker and Satanist Kenneth Anger, a disciple of the notorious occultist Aleister Crowley and an original member of Anton LaVey's Magic Circle from which the First Church of Satan evolved.[90] Jagger composed the Moog Synthesizer soundtrack for Anger's film *Invocation of My Demon Brother* and Richards played a role in his film *Lucifer Rising*. Based on Anger's advice, Jagger selected the devil from the tarot card pack designed by Aleister Crowley for the cover of their album, *Their Satanic Majesties Request*.[91]

Richards once noted in a *Rolling Stone* interview that the Stones' songs came spontaneously, like inspiration "at a séance." He described the songs as arriving "en masse," as if the Stones as song writers were only a willing and open "medium."[92] Alice Cooper allegedly claims that he received his name "from a spirit that possessed him during a séance." His song "Cold Ethyl" is about a love affair with a female corpse.[93]

Many additional rock stars have been involved in occultic practices which describe their musical inspiration in terms that suggest spirit possession and/or inspiration.[94]

Increasing numbers of other musicians are showing an interest in the occult, witchcraft, and occasionally even Satanism. Among the "black metal" groups, names that seem to indicate at least some interest in the occult are "Coven," "Dark Angel," "Demon," "Infernal Majesty," "Possessed," "Satan," "Cloven Hoof," and others. Jane's Addiction's singer Perry Farrell has been involved in saternia (witchcraft) ritual.[95]

Ozzy Osbourne noted, "I never seem to know exactly what I'm gonna do next. I just like to do what the spirits make me do. That way, I always have someone or something to blame."[96] Osbourne, an ex-lead singer for Black Sabbath, actually gave an altar-call for Satan while playing in Canada. He confesses, "Sometimes I feel like a medium for some outside force...."[97] Black Sabbath has also made altar calls to Lucifer at some of their concerts.[98] In "Master of Reality" they sing that he is "lord of this world" and "your confessor now."

According to a *Rolling Stone* interview, Peter Criss, the first and most famous drummer of the rock band KISS stated, "I believe in the devil as much as God. You can use either one to get things done."[99]

Members of the group Iron Maiden openly admit that they are dabbling in the occult, including witchcraft.[100] One Iron Maiden concert in Portland, Oregon, opened with the words "Welcome to Satan's sanctuary." Glenn Tipton of the group Judas Priest confessed that when he goes on stage, he goes crazy: "It's like someone else takes over my body."[101]

In describing what a Van Halen concert is like, David Lee Roth commented, "I'm gonna abandon my spirit to them [emotions], which is actually what I attempt to do. You work yourself up into that state and you fall in supplication of the demon gods."[102]

Guitarist Mick Mars of Motley Crüe described his band as "demonic, that's what we are."[103] Nikki Sixx referring to their "Shout at the Devil" stage show commented, "We have skulls, pentagrams, and all kinds of satanic symbols on stage.... I've always flirted with the devil."[104]

Stevie Nicks of Fleetwood Mac has several times dedicated their concerts to the witches of the world. An album of the rock group Venom entitled, "Welcome to Hell" contains the following words on the back cover. "We are possessed by all that is evil. The death of your God we demand: we spit at the virgin you worship, and sit at the Lord Satan's left hand." The "Rune" album of Led Zeppelin displays on the cover the famous black occultist Aleister Crowley. Led Zeppelin's Jimmy Page, allegedly a self-confessed Satanist, actually bought Crowley's old mansion. John Bonham, a drummer for the band, died in the house in 1980; Robert Plant allegedly split the group up after his death and blamed Page's obsession with the occult for his death.[105]

But according to the Bible, these occult practices are dangerous and to be avoided. (In our booklet *The Facts on the Occult* we have documented this.) Anyone who advocates doing them is rebelling against God. In the Bible God warns against occult involvement:

> Let no one be found among you ... who practices divination or sorcery, interprets omens, engages in witchcraft, or spells, or who is a medium or spiritist or

who consults the dead. Anyone who does these things is detestable to the Lord (Deuteronomy 18:9-12).

No one can deny that rock music has become a vehicle for promoting occultic practices. Consider again the common themes found in rock music: the use of illegal drugs, rebellion against authority, amoralism, nihilism, escapism, sexual license of all types, violence, the pursuit of the occult. Are these the kinds of philosophies that the spirit world would like to promote? A study of the history of the occult reveals only one answer.

– 9 –

How Can You Be a Discerning Listener?
by Robert Gerow

When someone asks for an opinion about music, it is frequently in connection with the "evils of Rock-and-Roll."

Though "Rock" may be the form of music which some folks find most offensive, the principles for evaluating it are the same as those for evaluating any form of music.

Our primary reaction to all music is emotional and not rational. Therefore, any proper evaluation must take place on two levels: First, "How does the music make me feel?" And, secondly, "What are the particulars of the lyrics, style, and mechanics of the composition in question?"

On the emotional level, it is just as possible for a listener to get "carried away" by a waltz, by "Middle-of-the-Road" music, or by Country & Western tunes, as it is by Rock-and-Roll. It could be self-pity that one form arouses, or nihilism or apathy stirred up by another, or erotic interests in a third. The danger can be present in all forms.

On a rational level, care also must be taken. The lyrics of a Country & Western tune may do as much harm to a middle-ager as the lyrics of a Rock-and-Roll song will do to his pre-adolescent. The "beautiful" melody of the latest Gospel song may hide theologically-incorrect lyrics. And the relaxing MOR ("Middle-of-the-Road") format may in fact be the vehicle for communicating a view that is contrary to moral principle.

So what shall we do?

Whatever the form or style of music, the discerning listener must...

1) *Evaluate the lyrics for content.* Much of what is marketed under the "Country & Western" format these days includes stories of unfaithfulness in marriages or between "lovers." Frequently, "Rock" lyrics are verbal orgies designed to incite or satisfy the basest of human interests. Frequently, "Contemporary" music will communicate a worldview which may be quite different from your own.

The discerning listener will pay attention to the words of the music he listens to. It has been said that "If you want to know where a culture is going, listen to its music." Doing so may be frightening. Not everyone is willing to make the effort to examine it that carefully. But if the music we listen to is written by folks with values different from our own, the least we should do is be aware of it and guard against being influenced unduly by it.

2) *Evaluate your emotional response.* What is the tune's overall effect on my way of thinking and responding to the world around me? The response to music is primarily emotional. The music we listen to "creates a mood." If a relationship has just "gone wrong," certain kinds of music will simply underscore the fact that you're feeling sorry for yourself. Music listened to without understanding can easily become an escape route to avoid dealing with circumstances and facing the future in some healthy way.

Volume and beat—another target for rock-and-roll music detractors—can also create a mood. It is almost hypnotic at times. But some of the "quieter" tunes can also be. The listener needs to be aware of this hypnotic effect, particularly in view of the lyrics that accompany it. In some cases it may border on a subtle form of "brainwashing." A tune will stick in our minds. To re-live the "mood" the tune evokes, we learn and repeat lyrics contrary to our own values.

3) *Balance your thinking about music.* It's entirely possible for other folks to have different tastes in music than we do without being "wrong." It is possible for someone to thoroughly enjoy "Christian Rock" while you have no place for it yourself. Someone else may prefer a Gregorian chant or some "mystical sounding stuff," while a third person may choose the classics or Western music. Nor is there anything wrong with a listener who is thoroughly fascinated by the old traditional music, secular or religious, as an expression

of what is meaningful in his life and as a source of enjoyment. Music is one of those areas in which there are almost as many views as there are folks who express them.

4) *Don't be afraid to enjoy your preferred musical style(s)*. If you are a discerning listener, then you don't need to be afraid of the emotional impact that your favorite music has on you. Songs of joy, praise, memories, favorite stories, and so on can become an important part of the fabric of your life. The role and function of music is to honor God and to refresh the soul of man. For the discerning listener this can be accomplished in a wide variety of musical styles.

Notes

1. *USA Today*, Oct. 11, 1985.
2. Ibid.
3. Videos correspond topically to chapters 2–7 and may be ordered from The John Ankerberg Show, P.O. Box 8977, Chattanooga, Tennessee 37411. Or call 1-615-892-7722, M–F, 8:30 A.M.–4:30 P.M. EST. Two earlier series are also available, The Dangers of Rock Music, Series I and Series II, discussing such additional topics as death, the occult, backmasking, Christianity and rebellion.
4. Rhoda Thomas Tripp, comp., *The International Thesaurus of Quotations* (New York: Thomas Y. Crowell, 1970), p. 419.
5. Ibid.
6. Jacques Barzun, *Darwin, Marx, Wagner* (Garden City, NY: Anchor, 1959), p. 244.
7. Tripp, *International Thesaurus*, p. 420.
8. Ralph L. Woods, comp. and ed., *The World Treasury of Religious Quotations* (New York: Garland Books, 1966), p. 660.
9. Tripp, *International Thesaurus*, p. 419.
10. *Life* magazine, June 28, 1968.
11. Eric Holmberg, *The Hell's Bells Study Guide* (Gainesville, FL: Reel to Real, 1990), p. 10.
12. Ibid.
13. Ibid., citing *Life* magazine, June 28, 1968.
14. Pythagoras and Plato citations are from David A. Noebel, *The Marxist Minstrels* (Tulsa, OK: American Christian College Press, 1974), p. 4.
15. Ibid., citing *Politics*, 1339a, 1340b.
16. Citations are from Tripp, *International Thesaurus*, p. 418; Woods, *The World Treasury*, p. 659.
17. Ibid.
18. Ibid.
19. Ibid., cf. Allan Bloom, *The Closing of the American Mind* (New York: Simon and Schuster, 1987), pp. 68-81.
20. Hannelore Wass, et. al., "Adolescents' Interest in and Views of Destructive Themes in Rock Music," *Omega*, vol. 19, no. 3, p. 182; Susan Baker, cofounder of Parents' Music Resource Center (PMRC) in *Let's Talk Rock: A Primer for Parents* (Nashville, 1990), p. 9.
21. Ted Schwarz and Duane Empey, *Satanism: Is Your Family Safe?* (Grand Rapids, MI: Zondervan, 1989), p. 151-52.
22. Howard C. Nielson, member of Congress, letter dated April 19, 1990.
23. Wass, et. al., "Adolescents' Interest," p. 178.
24. Copy of legislative proposal, 101st Congress, 2nd Session, with concurrent resolution attached by Howard C. Nielson, member of Congress, 42390-1.
25. Elizabeth F. Brown and William Hendee, "Adolescents and Their Music: Insights into the Health of Adolescents," *Journal of the American Medical Association*, Sept. 22/29, 1989, p. 1659.
26. Bloom, *Closing of the American Mind*, pp. 73-76.
27. Brown and Hendee, "Adolescents and Their Music," p. 1659.
28. In *Media Update*, July/Aug. 1989, citing a survey of 1,120 youth, reported in *The San Diego Union*, Mar. 8, 1989, p. 6, available from Media Update, P.O. Box 969, Cardiff, CA 92007-0969.
29. From Wass, et. al., "Adolescents' Interest," p. 185; cf. H. Stipp, "Children's Knowledge of and Taste in Popular Music," *Popular Music and Society*, vol. 10, 1985, pp. 1-15.
30. *Media Update*, Nov./Dec. 1989, pp. 2-3.
31. *USA Today*, Oct. 11, 1985.

32. *Media Update*, Sep./Oct. 1989, pp. 1-2.
33. E.g., *Rolling Stone* article on "Skid Row" (Sept. 19, 1991); *Spin* articles on "Metallica" (Oct. 1991; cf. p. 40), Sinéad O'Connor (Nov. 1991, cf. "Fear of Music"); *Groundswell* (Hawaii) article on "Jane's Addiction" (July-Aug. 1991).
34. *Globe*, June 6, 1985, p. 37.
35. Nikki Sixx in *Metal Studs Special*, no. 20, p. 21.
36. Ibid.
37. Pat Blashill, "Between Rock and an Art Place," *Details for Men: The Music Issue*, July 1991, pp. 98, 100.
38. Brown and Hendee, "Adolescents and Their Music," p. 1662.
39. Bloom, *Closing of the American Mind*, pp. 73-74.
40. Part of this "Things to Think About" section is exerpted from Eric Holmberg, *The Hell's Bells Study Guide*.
41. "Sharp Rise in Rare Sex Related Diseases," *New York Times*, July 14, 1988; Lewis J. Lord, "Sex With Care," *U.S. News and World Report*, June 2, 1968; cf. Josh McDowell, *The Myths of Sex Education* (San Bernardino, CA: Here's Life, 1990).
42. *Rolling Stone*, Aug. 22, 1991, p. 15.
43. Wass, et al., "Adolescents' Interest," p. 179; Brown and Hendee, "Adolescents and Their Music," p. 1662; Dr. Marty Tingelhoff, *Documentation of Exposé on Rock and Roll, Soul and Country Music*, n.p.p.: Living Word Spoken Ministries, Aug. 1987, p. 8; *Time*, Mar. 19, 1990. Special thanks to Dr. Tingelhoff.
44. Wass, et al., "Adolescents' Interest," p. 182.
45. In *USA Today*, Oct. 11, 1985, p. 10A.
46. Ibid.
47. Baker, *Let's Talk Rock*, pp. 7-8.
48. Paul King, "Heavy Metal Music and Drug Use in Adolescents," *Postgraduate Medicine*, April 1988, p. 297.
49. In an MTV interview, Osbourne said the song is *anti*-suicide; that he never intended it to encourage suicide. But a straightforward reading of the lyrics reveals that it does advocate suicide. When pressed on certain lyrics, some artists may refer to "levels of meaning" in their songs in an attempt to diffuse criticism.
50. Wass, et al., "Adolescents' Interest," p. 186, sampled 700 adolescents. The themes were homicide, suicide, and Satanism. Cf. Aerosmith's "Janie's Got a Gun."
51. Information from Parents' Music Resource Center, Nashville, TN, 1990.
52. Arthur Lyons, *Satan Wants You* (New York: Mysterious Press, 1988), p. 171.
53. Schwarz and Empey, *Satanism: Is Your Family Safe?* p. 154.
54. Cf. Dave Hart, "Heavy Metal Madness," *Media Update*, July/Aug. 1989, p. 5.
55. Ibid.
56. Brown and Hendee, "Adolescents and Their Music," p. 1661.
57. Ibid., p. 1662.
58. Wass, et al., "Adolescents' Interest,"; King, "Heavy Metal Music."
59. Brown and Hendee, "Adolescents and Their Music," p. 1662.
60. *Time*, May 7, 1990, pp. 92-94.
61. John Cale, recalling his days with Velvet Underground described their philosophy as "Give people hard drugs. Give them the drugs they want. Acid? Give 'em heroin." found in *Spin*, May 1990 interview, p. 30.
62. King, "Heavy Metal Music"; cf. Wass, et al., "Adolescents' Interest," p. 82.
63. Cliff Linedecker, *Country Music Stars and the Supernatural* (New York: Dell, 1979).
64. In *People*, Sept. 3, 1979.
65. Marty Tingelhoff, Dr., *Documentation of Exposé on Rock and Roll, Soul and Country Music*, n.p.p.: Living Word Spoken Ministries, Aug. 1987, p. 18.
66. *The Gainesville Sun*, Aug. 10, 1990, p. 3 of "Scene" section.
67. *Spin*, June 1990, p. 59.
68. *Time*, July 30, 1990, p. 68.
69. Dave Hart review in *Media Update*, Sept.–Oct. 1990, p. 12.
70. "Thanks to the Almighty Creator" appears on the back of their "Hangin' Tough" album. Thousands of yearning fans have seized this flimsy evidence as proof that the New Kids are Christians. But you can hardly find a rap album or a music awards ceremony today where someone isn't thanking God; even the artists who are singing about the most vile sexual perversions. Generic titles for God (unfortunately "God" itself has become generic) like "Creator," "the Man upstairs," "Higher Power," and so on mean little without theological content and actions behind them.
71. David Tame, *The Secret Power of Music* (Rochester, VT: Destiny Books, 1984), p. 152.
72. Cf. "Red Hot Chili Peppers," "Hole Lotta Love," "Corrosion of Conformity," "Consolidated Trust."
73. "Jane's Addiction," *Groundswell* (Hawaii), July/Aug. 1991, p. 50.
74. *Spin* magazine, June 1990, p. 18.
75. David Crosby, interview, *Rolling Stone* magazine, vol. 1, p. 410.
76. In Tingelhoff, *Documentation of Exposé*, p. 4.
77. Ibid., p. 5.
78. *Metal Edge*, Aug. 1987, p. 12; cf. p. 10.
79. In Tingelhoff, *Documentation of Exposé*, p. 6.
80. *Rock Beat*, 1987, p. 41.
81. In Tingelhoff, *Documentation of Exposé*, p. 7.
82. Bloom, *Closing of the American Mind*, p. 72.
83. Ibid., p. 77.

84. *Rock* magazine, June 1984, p. 322.
85. *Rolling Stone*, Dec. 2, 1979, p. 35.
86. *Spin*, Nov. 1991, p. 51.
87. *Creem Metal*, Mar. 1986, p. 12.
88. John Lennon, *A Spaniard in the Works* (New York: Simon and Schuster, 1965), p. 14.
89. Dave Hunt, *America: The Sorcerer's New Apprentice* (Eugene, OR: Harvest House, 1988), pp. 239-40.
90. Arthur Lyons, *Satan Wants You*, p. 88.
91. Ibid., p. 167.
92. Bob Larson, *Larson's Book of Rock* (Wheaton, IL: Tyndale, 1987), p. 138.
93. *Moody Monthly*, Sept. 1982, p. 34.
94. Larson, *Larson's Book of Rock*, pp. 125-35; Hunt, *America: The Sorcerer's New Apprentice*, pp. 245-46.
95. *Details for Men*, July 1991, pp. 100-101.
96. *Faces* magazine, Nov. 1983, p. 24.
97. Tingelhoff, *Documentation of Exposé*, p. 21.
98. Ibid.
99. *Rolling Stone*, Jan. 12, 1978.
100. *Creem*, Sept. 1982.
101. *Hit Parade*, Fall 1984.
102. *Rock*, April 1984.
103. *Heavy Metal Times*, May 1983.
104. *Circus*, Jan. 31, 1984.
105. Tingelhoff, *Documentation of Exposé*, p. 25.

Select Bibliography

Ankerberg, John and Weldon, John. 1991. *The Facts on the Occult*. Eugene, OR: Harvest House. 1. Ankerberg, John, Holmberg, Eric, and Weldon, John. 1991. *Rock Music's Powerful Messages*, book 2 by Eric Holmberg. 2. Barnard, Stephen. *Rock: An Illustrated History*. 3. Bloom, Allan. "Music" in *The Closing of the American Mind*. 4. Breskin, David. 1984. Kids in the Dark (satanic killing). *Rolling Stone*, Nov. 22. 5. Brown, Elizabeth F. and Hendee, William. 1989. Adolescents and Their Music: Insights into the Health of Adolescents. *Journal of the American Medical Association*, Sept. 22/29. 6. Brown, Rosemary. 1971. *Unfinished Symphonies*. New York: William Morrow. 7. Committee on Communications, American Academy of Pediatrics. 1989. 8. The Impact of Rock Lyrics and Music Videos on Children and Youth. *Pediatrics*, 83:314-315. 9. Congressional Hearing. 1987. Song Lyrics. 10. Davis, S. 1985. Pop Lyrics: A Mirror and Molder of Society. *Et cetera*, Summer. 11. Fielden, Thomas. *Music and Character*. 12. Gilman and Paperte. *Music and Your Emotions*. 13. Greenfield, P.M., Bruzzone, L., et. al. 1987. What Is Rock Music Doing to the Minds of Our Youth? A First Experimental Look at the Effects of Rock Music. *Journal of Early Adolescence*, 7:315-29. 14. Grout, Donald J. *A History of Western Music*. 15. Halpern, Steven. *Sound Health: The Music and Sounds that Make Us Whole*. 16. Hender, Herb. *Year by Year in the Rock Era: Events and Conditions Shaping the Rock Generations that Reshaped America*. 17. Hunt, Dave. 1988. Satanism, Rock and Rebellion. *America: The Sorcerer's New Apprentice*. Eugene, OR: Harvest House. 18. King, Paul. April 1988. "Heavy Metal Music and Drug Use in Adolescents." *Postgraduate Medicine*. 19. Lang, Paul Henry. *Music and Western Civilization*. 20. Larson, Bob. 1987. *Larson's Book of Rock*. Wheaton, IL: Tyndale. 21. Long, Albert. 1988. *A Long Look at Hard Rock Music*. Waco, TX: Word. 22. Machlis, Joseph. *Introduction to Contemporary Music*. 23. Marsh, Dave. *Rocktopicon: Unlikely Questions and Their Surprising Answers*. 24. National Institute of Mental Health. 1982. *Television and Behavior: Ten Years of Scientific Progress and Implication for the 80s: Summary Report*. Washington, D.C.: Department of Health and Human Services. 25. Nielson, Howard C. Submitted resolution to House of Representatives. 101st Congress, Second Session. 26. Parents' Music Resource Center. 1990. *Let's Talk Rock: A Primer for Parents*. Nashville, TN. 27. Pidgeon, John. *Rock and Roll Babylon*. 28. Portnoy, Julius. *Music in the Life of Man*. 29. Prinsky, L. and Rosenbaum, J. 1987. Leer-ics or Lyrics?: Teenage Impressions of Rock and Roll. *Youth Society* 18:384-396. 30. Riese, Randall and Hitchens, Neil. *Nashville Babylon: The Uncensored Truth and Private Lives of Country Music's Greatest Stars*. 31. Routh, Francis. *Contemporary Music: An Introduction*. 32. Schwarz, Ted and Empey, Duane. Devil Songs: Rock and Roll? *Satanism: Is Your Family Safe?* 33. Scott, Cyril. *Music: Its Secret Influence Throughout the Ages*. 34. _____. *The Influence of Music on History and Morals*. 35. _____. *The Philosophy of Modernism in Connection with Music*. 36. Tame, David. *The Secret Power of Music*. 37. Tingelhoff, Dr. Marty. 1987. *Documentation of Exposé on Rock and Roll, Soul and Country Music*. Ms. n.p.p. Living Word Spoken Ministries. 38. Walker, J.R. 1987. How Viewing of MTV Relates to Exposure of Other Media Violence. *Journalism Quarterly*. 64:756-762. 39. Wellesz, Egon, ed. *Ancient and Oriental Music. The New Oxford History of Music*, vol. 1. 40. White, Timothy. *Rock Lives: Profiles and Interviews*. 41. Yates, Peter. *Twentieth Century Music*.